SCHOLASTIC

Best of Dr. Jean

Science & Math

More Than 100 Delightful, Skill-Building Ideas and Activities for Early Learners

by Dr. Jean Feldman

Counting & Estimating

Shapes, Sizes & Patterns

Addition & Subtraction

Time, Money & Measurement

NEW YORK • TORONTO • LONDON • AUCKLAND • SYDNEY
MEXICO CITY • NEW DELHI • HONG KONG • BUENOS AIRES

Teaching *Resources*

To Mrs. Myers, my kindergarten and first-grade teacher

She made me feel special and she made coming to school
the most exciting thing in my life!

My wish is that the activities in this book will instill
the same love of learning in your students!

Cover illustration by Brenda Sexton
Cover and interior design by Holly Grundon
Illustration by Milk and Cookies
ISBN: 0-439-59725-0
Copyright © 2005 by Dr. Jean Feldman
Published by Scholastic Inc.
All rights reserved.
Printed in the U.S.A.

9 10   40   13 12 11 10 09 08

Contents

Introduction

Welcome to
Best of Dr. Jean
Science & Math

The worlds of science and math are rich with opportunities for exploration, discovery, and wonderment. Within these pages, you'll find countless ways to invite young children into these worlds and tap into their natural curiosity. At the same time, you'll be meeting the standards. (See pages 6 and 29 for more.)

The phrase "children learn by doing" is particularly true with math and science. Young children don't think abstractly, so they need multiple experiences with hands-on materials to construct concepts about numbers and the world around them. Open your eyes to daily opportunities for learning math and science on the playground, as you read a story, as children work in centers, or as you talk informally. Stretch their vocabulary and thinking skills with questions such as:

* "Why do you think so?"
* "What made you say that?"
* "How did you know that?"
* "How might you find out?"
* "What do you think will happen?"
* "Why do you think that happened?"

And remember to share children's joy of learning as you facilitate positive experiences that will influence lifelong attitudes about mathematics and the sciences!

Introduction

Science

The first half of this book focuses on bringing science to life in your classroom. You'll find tons of ideas for creating a science center; step-by-step, simple experiments; and all sorts of science "surprises" to spark children's interest and challenge their thinking. Children will explore seasons, magnets, plants, the five senses, colors, nature, and more. You'll also find strategies for integrating reading and writing along the way! As you learn together, you'll be helping children develop skills in

- discovering
- researching
- observing
- predicting
- planning
- classifying
- exploring
- questioning
- communicating
- experimenting
- analyzing

Math

Children will catch "math fever" with the exciting hands-on activities presented in the second half of this book. You'll learn how to sing math, move math, eat math, and make math more meaningful and fun! You'll also find ideas for simple games and materials, as well as suggestions for setting up a math center. Take a look at some of the concepts and skills you'll be building:

- one-to-one correspondence
- matching sets and numerals
- counting
- writing numerals
- patterns
- shapes
- classifying
- money
- measurement
- time
- estimation
- graphs
- addition and subtraction

Science Center Tips

- Rotate materials frequently to maintain children's interest.
- Encourage children to bring in their own "treasures" from nature. Have them explain what they know about their natural items to classmates. Ask, *Who else knows something about this?*

The science explorations in this book lay the foundation for children's deeper understanding of concepts later on. For instance, children might not understand that a chemical reaction between vinegar and copper cleans pennies, but they can observe, compare, and describe what they see during the experiment. Simple explanations are provided for your own background, but young children will benefit more from concrete observations rather than abstract explanations.

Setting Up a **Science Center**

So much can happen in a science center—discovery, exploration, observation, prediction, communication, experimentation—all in one little area of the room!

Materials: You'll want to stock your science center with all sorts of child-safe items:

* aquarium
* balance scale
* blocks
* classroom pets
* color paddles
* encyclopedia
* feathers
* "feely" sock
* field guides
* flashlight

* flowers, petals, plant pieces
* kaleidoscope
* leaves
* magnets
* magnifying glass
* mirror
* models (dinosaurs, insects, and so on)
* nonfiction books on science topics
* paper, pencils, clipboards
* plants

* posters and pictures
* prism
* rocks and pebbles
* sand
* science magazines
* seeds
* shells
* simple machines
* soil
* stethoscope
* terrarium
* thermometer (child-safe)

Meeting the Science Standards

The activities in this section align with the guidelines and teaching practices set out by the National Academy of Sciences' *National Science Education Standards* (1996), which recommend that children:

Children:
* Ask questions about objects, organisms, and events in the environment
* Plan and conduct simple investigations
* Employ simple equipment and tools to gather data and extend the senses
* Use data to construct a reasonable explanation
* Communicate investigations and explanations

Content Standards Covered:
* recognizing observable properties
* grouping by properties
* changes in the state of matter
* motion
* basic needs of plants and animals
* characteristics of organisms
* life cycles
* patterns in weather over time
* describing weather in measurable terms
* recognizing characteristics of the seasons
* using tools to enhance observation
* using tools to measure

Discovery Bottles

Children can explore so many science concepts independently with discovery bottles. They're also inexpensive and simple to make! Children are captivated by them, plus they're great for calming the group down and getting their attention at circle time.

Materials: Clean, clear (not cloudy or green) plastic bottles in all shapes and sizes (you might ask families to donate them). Any size or type will do: soda bottles, shampoo bottles, water bottles, bulk food jars, and so on. Sixteen-ounce bottles are easiest for young children to manipulate. You'll also need a glue gun for making most of these.

How To:

1. Remove the labels by soaking the bottles in warm water. Use Goo Gone, mineral spirits, or baby oil to remove the stickiness. You can also use a hair dryer to remove the labels (do not use any water, simply blow hot air on them, and they will peel off)!

2. Try one or more of the ideas on these pages (pages 7–9). Dollar stores and craft stores are great places to find materials. The Oriental Trading Company (www.orientaltrading.com) is another great source for inexpensive, small items.

3. Seal the lids with a glue gun to make the bottles watertight. Store the bottles in a plastic crate, or line them up on a bookshelf in the science center.

Smell & Tell

Poke holes in a bottle (a nail or ice pick works well). Fill with potpourri and invite children to describe the scent. You can also soak cotton balls with cooking extracts (vanilla, mint, almond), or add other spices, and put them in different bottles for a guessing game. Have children close their eyes and smell. Ask, *What does the smell remind you of? What do you think it is?*

Ocean Bottle

Pour a half cup of sand in a bottle. Add small shells and a tiny toy fish (you can use a small uninflated balloon for a fish). Fill the bottle about two-thirds with water, then add a drop of blue food coloring and a little glitter. Invite children to visit the seashore! Ask, *What colors do you see? What shapes?*

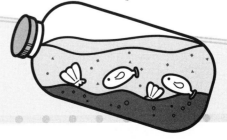

Static Bottle

Tear tissue paper and foam packing into small pieces and put them into a bottle. Rub the bottle briskly against the carpet, your hair, or wool clothing. Ask, *Why do you think the paper or foam sticks to the side of the bottle?* (Static electricity is created when you rub the bottle, causing the paper and foam to repel each other.)

Wave Bottle

Fill a bottle about two-thirds with water and add several drops of food coloring. Fill to the top with vegetable oil or baby oil. Invite children to slowly tilt the bottle to create waves. They can also shake it up and watch the oil coagulate on top.

Magnetic Bottle

Fill a bottle halfway with dry rice. Add objects that a magnet will attract, such as paper clips, pins, and nails. Attach a magnet to an 18-inch length of string, then challenge children to attract the objects. Also, put paper clips in a bottle of water (without rice).

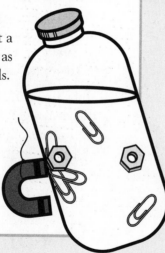

Dirty Bottle

Put one or two spoonfuls of dirt in a bottle. Fill halfway with water. Shake, then observe as the dirt settles. You might also collect dirt samples from different states, or collect sand from different beaches, and try using them in bottles. Label each bottle with the origin of its contents.

Bubble Bottle

Fill a bottle about one-third with water. Add a drop of detergent and a drop of food coloring. Ask children what they think will happen if it is shaken, then let them shake the bottle. Were their predictions correct? You might even experiment to see which brand of detergent makes the best bubbles!

Science

De-Stress Bottle

Put two tablespoons of crayon shavings in a bottle, then fill to the top with water. Children can shake up the bottle, then relax as they watch the crayon shavings float and sink! You can also add a little glitter to the mix for extra sparkle. This is great when a child needs a little downtime.

Tornado Bottle

Fill a bottle almost to the top with water. Add a tiny drop of detergent, one drop of food coloring, several small balls of aluminum foil, and plastic trees. Turn the bottle upside down, hold the neck, and quickly swirl it around until a funnel forms. This is similar to the way wind moves to create a tornado.

Magic Bottle

Fill a bottle with water and add several drops of food coloring. Sprinkle in a little Pearl Powder. (you can find this at craft stores near the soap-making ingredients). The lustrous pearl sparkle is absolutely magical when you swirl it around! Ask children to describe what they see. What does it remind them of?

Mystery Sound

Put one of the following in several different bottles (one type of material per bottle): dry rice, dry beans, unpopped corn, raw macaroni noodles, and so on. Cover the bottle with a sock. Have children shake and try to determine the contents. Adding a little water presents an extra challenge!

Habitat Bottles

For a desert habitat, fill a bottle halfway with sand. Add rocks and plastic lizards and snakes. For an arctic habitat, use cotton balls and small plastic arctic animals. For a swamp habitat, use water, dirt, silk greenery, and a small plastic alligator!

Scientist of the Day

Help children build responsibility—and see themselves as scientists.

Materials: white lab coat (or large button-down shirt with sleeves cut off), safety goggles or empty pair of glass frames (optional)

How To:

1. Each day (or week) select a different child to be Scientist of the Day. This child can be in charge of setting up, helping manage, and cleaning up the science center.

2. Invite the child to wear a white lab coat and help you demonstrate whatever experiment or exploration you have prepared for the center. If you have safety goggles, explain that scientists use these to stay safe.

3. Later, at circle time, invite the Scientist of the Day to summarize to the group what happened at the center.

Mirror, Mirror

Children explore the concepts of symmetry and reflection.

Materials: small handheld, child-safe mirrors; paper; crayons or markers; large index cards

How To:

1. Show children the mirror and the half images below (copy them onto large index cards with marker). Ask, *How can we make this picture complete?*

2. Demonstrate how to complete the pictures by placing the mirror on the edge of the image. Invite children to try it themselves.

3. Let children make their own designs on index cards with crayons or markers, and reflect them in the mirror.

And...

✳ Invite each child to write his or her name and hold a mirror to it to see it backward!

Color Paddles

Children experiment with primary and secondary colors.

Materials: six sturdy paper plates; scissors; stapler; clear acetate tinted red, yellow, and blue (often used for report covers, available at office supply stores)

How To:

1. Cut paper-plate-size circles from the acetate sheets. Cut the centers out of the plates and staple a different color of acetate between two paper plate rims so that you have three round "windows."

2. Invite children to experiment by looking through each color. Next, let them put two colors together and hold them up to the light. Invite them to walk around the room, seeing everything in a new color.

3. Encourage them to name the two colors they put together (primary colors) and the color they create when combined (secondary color).

And...

✳ Take three clear cups and fill them halfway with water. Add a few drops of red, blue, and yellow food coloring to the cups. Let children use eye droppers and mix the colors together (one color per cup) on wax paper or in a white ice cube tray.

✳ Give each child a cup of vanilla yogurt. Let children choose two colors of food coloring from a selection of three (red, yellow, or blue) and put a drop of each in the yogurt. Have them stir and see what happens! (For Halloween, add red and yellow food color to make orange yogurt. For St. Patrick's Day, add a drop of blue and a drop of yellow.)

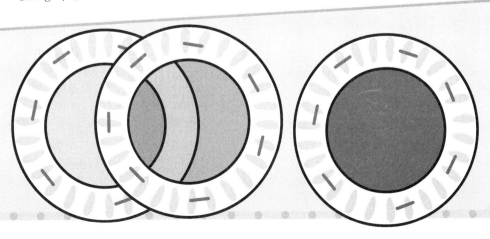

Shiny Pennies

Children observe chemical changes in familiar objects—pennies!

Materials: old pennies, half cup vinegar, one tablespoon salt, glass and spoon

How To:

1. Put a half cup of vinegar in the glass. Add one tablespoon salt and stir to dissolve.

2. Drop the pennies in the glass and stir them around while you count to 25 together with children.

3. Take the pennies out of the glass and rinse them in water.

4. Shiny pennies, just like magic! Ask, *What do you think made the pennies shiny? Will it work with nickels or dimes?* Explain that pennies contain copper, which darkens (oxidizes) as it is exposed to air. The vinegar and salt make the dark coating dissolve.

And...

✳ Set up an experiment station with three bowls. Put vinegar with salt in one bowl, ketchup in the second, and lemon juice in the third. Have children predict which one will shine the pennies best. Record their predictions, then carry out the experiment.

Pepper Scatter

Children love observing this classic experiment.

Materials: clear bowl, black pepper, liquid dish detergent

How To:

1. Fill the bowl with water. Sprinkle the pepper on top.

2. Squirt a drop of detergent in the middle of the bowl.

3. Observe! Ask, *What do you think makes the pepper scatter?* Explain that the soap changes the water at the middle and the pepper is drawn to the edge, rather than the middle.

And...

✳ Instead of detergent, dip a bar of soap into the bowl. What happens?

✳ Pour half a cup of room-temperature whole milk into a pie pan. Drop several different colors food coloring down the sides of the pan, then squirt a little detergent in the middle. What happens to the colors? Ask children to draw the steps to this experiment in sequential order.

Happy Face Balloon

Demonstrate chemical reactions and the concept of inflation.

Materials: large easily inflatable balloon, permanent marker, bottle, half cup vinegar, baking soda, spoon, funnel

How To:

1. Blow up the balloon but do not tie it. Have a volunteer pinch it closed so the air doesn't come out, and draw a happy face on it with the marker. Deflate.

2. Pour a half cup of vinegar in the bottle. Using the funnel, put several spoonfuls of baking soda into the balloon.

3. Hold the balloon so that the baking soda will not spill out. Stretch the balloon over the mouth of the bottle. Hold up the balloon so the baking soda falls in the bottle. Observe what happens.

4. Ask, *What made the balloon blow up?* Have children draw pictures in sequential order to show how this experiment was conducted. Explain that mixing the baking soda with vinegar causes a gas called carbon dioxide to be released. The gas expands and takes up space.

And...

* Demonstrate volcanic action with vinegar and baking soda. Set a cup inside a shallow pan. Put a half cup of vinegar in the cup and add a few drops of red food coloring. Add two tablespoons baking soda to the vinegar and stir. Volcano!

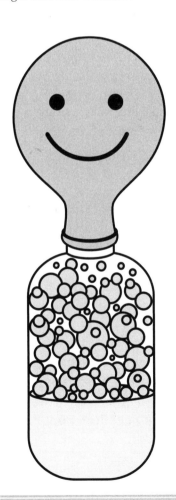

Bubble, Bubble, Pop!

Whether children are blowing bubbles themselves or observing you, this is sure to mesmerize!

Materials: pie pan, Joy dish detergent, one-quarter cup glycerin (available in drugstores), 10 cups water, pipe cleaner

How To:

1. Mix the ingredients in a large pie pan.

2. Allow the mixture to sit at room temperature for one hour.

3. Make a bubble wand by forming a circle from a pipe cleaner. Demonstrate how to use the wand. Invite children to blow bubbles!

And...

✳ Blow bubbles with flyswatters, plastic rings from drink cans, or berry baskets.

✳ Try using your hands to blow bubbles! Make a circle with your index finger and thumb. Dip in the solution, then blow.

✳ Sing this song to the tune of "Ten Little Indians." Hold up fingers as you count:

> One little, two little, three little bubbles.
> Four little, five little, six little bubbles.
> Seven little, eight little, nine little bubbles.
> Pop! Pop! Pop! Pop! Pop! (Clap hands on each *pop*.)

Marvelous Magnets

Children predict, sort, and classify as they explore the concept of magnetism.

Materials: magnets (one per child if possible), box of small metallic (iron containing) and nonmetallic materials (paper clips, crayons, fastened safety pins, plastic toys, toothpicks, tissues, pennies, dimes, and so on)

How To:

1. Invite each child to use a magnet to pick up each object.

2. Have children sort the objects by category: things the magnet will attract and things it does not attract.

3. Ask, *How are the objects that the magnet attracts alike? How about the objects that the magnet does not attract?*

And...

* Let children walk around the room and find other objects that the magnet will attract.

* Offer children several different types of magnets, such as a horseshoe, bar, circle, magnetic strip, and refrigerator magnet.

* Give children each a paper plate. Have them place a paper clip on top. Show them how to slide the magnet under the plate and make the paper clip move!

* Fill a cup with water. Put paper clips in the water. Ask, *Do you think the magnet can attract the paper clips through the water?*

* Put iron filings, paper clips, or magnetic letters in the sand table. Have children go on a treasure hunt and find them with a magnet.

Funnel Phone

Children explore concepts of sound as they observe their own sense of hearing.

Materials: two plastic funnels, a four- to eight-inch length of plastic tubing $^3/_8$-inch thick (available at hardware stores), duct tape

How To:

1. Fit each end of the plastic tubing in each funnel and tape in place.

2. Have one child hold a funnel to his or her ear while another child talks into the other funnel. Ask, *How does sound get from one funnel to the next?* Explain that the sounds of our voices create vibrations called sound waves. These waves travel through the tube and are magnified by the funnel.

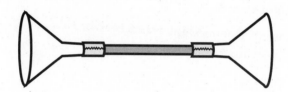

And...

✳ Make individual phones with paper cups, string, and paper clips. Poke holes in the bottom of two cups and thread the string through the holes. Tie a paper clip to the ends of the string to keep them in the bottom of the cup. Children take turns speaking and listening with the "cup phones."

✳ Have children cup their ears with their hands and say their names aloud, then say their names without their hands to their ears. Can they hear the difference in volume?

✳ Make a "clucker" with a plastic cup, a 20-inch length of string, and a paper clip. Poke a hole in the bottom of the cup. Thread the string through the hole and tie a paper clip to the end of the string in the cup. Hold the cup and pull on the string. Now, wet the string in a cup of water and pull on it with a jerking motion. It will sound like a hen clucking! Ask, *How does the sound change when the string is wet?* (Moisture makes the string vibrate more easily, increasing sound.)

Cluck!

Helicopters

Here's a simple physics experiment that amazes children.

Materials: paper, scissors, paper clips

How To:

1. Cut a paper helicopter for each child using the pattern below.

2. Distribute and then demonstrate how to cut as indicated and then fold the top flaps in opposite directions. Fold in the two sides and attach the paper clip to the bottom. Hold it high in the air and let it go. Say, *Describe how it moves. Can you think of anything in nature that flies like these helicopters?*

And...

✳ Demonstrate the concept of gravity by putting a book in one hand and the paper helicopter in another. Ask, *Which one will fly better? Why?* Have children observe the differences.

✳ Make five different helicopters: one from construction paper, one from tagboard, one from tissue paper, one from cardboard, and one from newsprint. Place the five different helicopters on the chalkboard ledge and have children each write their name above the one they think will fly best. Test each helicopter and number them from best to worst. *Why do you think ____ flew better than ____?*

✳ Make paper airplanes and see whose can fly the farthest.

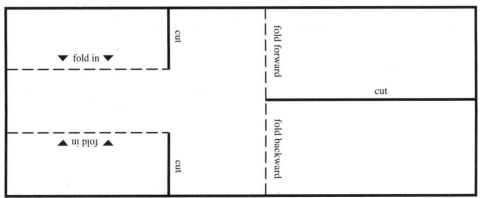

Five Senses

Invite children to pay special attention to each of their five senses.

How To:

1. Teach children this song about their five senses. Sing it to the tune of "BINGO."

2. Try some of the activities on these pages (pages 18–20).

> I have five senses that I use
>
> to help me learn each day.
>
> See, hear, smell, taste, and touch.
>
> See, hear, smell, taste, and touch.
>
> See, hear, smell, taste, and touch.
>
> I use them every day.

Touch

* Take several pairs of old socks. Put a different small object in the toe of each (ball, block, crayon, spoon, toy car, sponge, coin, and so on). Knot the top of each. Have children feel the sock and guess what is inside.

* Have children take off their shoes and sit at a table, then invite them to identify different objects on the floor with their feet!

* Slide a plastic cup into an old sock. Put objects with unusual textures in the cup (dog biscuit, dryer lint, key, and so on). Ask children to reach into the sock, put their hands into the cup, and try to identify the objects.

* Make a "Please Touch" book by gluing samples of different textures onto each page and writing sentences to describe them. For example: *This is rough.* (sandpaper) *This is bumpy.* (bubblewrap) *This is smooth.* (satin) *This is scratchy.* (burlap) *This is soft.* (cotton ball)

* Take a walk outside and identify different textures in nature. Ask, *Can you find something sticky? Soft? Hard? Rough?*

Taste

Ask each child to bring a fruit, vegetable, bread, cheese, or other healthy food for a tasting party. (Ask families to cut foods into the number of pieces you will need for everyone.) Which foods are sweet? Salty? Sour? Bitter? Choose one food to represent each taste, then make a graph of everyone's favorite food.

Sweet	Salty	Sour	Bitter
|||	||||	||	|

Smell

Gather film canisters or similar containers. In each, put an object with a distinguishing smell, such as cinnamon, cocoa, baby powder, coffee grounds, a lemon slice, and so on. Put a cotton ball on top so you can't see the object. Put on the lids. Mix up the containers, then have children close their eyes, open, smell, and identify what is in each.

Hearing

✳ Gather ten empty film containers. Put dry rice in two of them, beans in two, pennies in two, paper clips in two, and salt in two. Put on the tops and mix them up. Have children try to match the containers that have the same items by shaking them and matching sounds. (Put matching stickers on the bottoms of pairs so children can self-check.)

✳ Have children close their eyes as you walk around the room making various sounds (turn on the water, scoot a chair, write on the board, open the door, use the pencil sharpener, and so on). See if they can identify what you are doing.

✳ Go outside and sit in a comfortable area. Ask children to close their eyes for one minute and listen. Tell them to remember all the sounds they hear. Make a list of the sounds when you return to the classroom.

Sight

Cut a paper towel roll in half and tape the two halves together, side by side. Punch a hole in the top of each roll and tie a piece of string through the holes. (Make sure the string is long enough to go easily over children's heads.) Let children decorate the binoculars with markers or crayons. Have children look out the window, then describe what they see. You can even cover the ends of the rolls with colored cellophane to make special binoculars! Encourage children to talk about how the colored cellophane changes what they see.

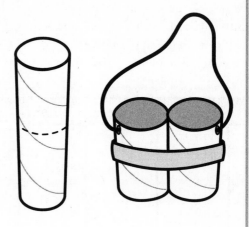

And...

✴ Draw two large circles on a sheet of paper and write "I saw _____." Copy for each child. Take children on a nature walk with their binoculars. Back in the classroom, have them draw what they saw as if they were looking through binoculars. Help them complete the sentence, then bind their pages together into a book.

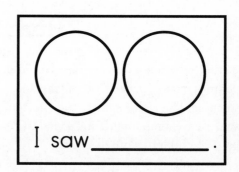

I saw_____.

✴ Place a pair of real binoculars on a table by a window. Add a notebook, pencil, crayons, and markers. Let children observe with the binoculars and draw and write what they see.

Bird Feeders

Children love caring for birds—and observing them.

Materials: plastic milk jug, birdseed, scissors, yarn or twine

How To:

1. Cut a hole in the side of the milk jug with scissors. (An adult will need to do this.)

2. Tie a piece of yarn or twine to the top of the milk jug for a hanger.

3. Put one cup of birdseed in the bottom of the jug, then hang it on a tree as close to a classroom window as possible.

4. Put a pair of binoculars and a bird identification book near the bird feeder and encourage children to identify the birds that feed there!

And...

✳ Ask, *Why is it important to feed the birds in the winter?* Remind children that birds need water as well as food. *How can we give birds water? How are all birds the same? How are they different?*

✳ Put out other foods (cracker crumbs, dry cereal, raisins, and so on) and record which ones the birds like best.

✳ In the spring, weave bits of string, yarn, or straw in a berry basket or onion bag for birds to use in building nests.

✳ Let children make other bird feeders. (Be aware of peanut allergies some children may have. Substitute honey or lard for peanut butter.)

　❄ String o-shaped cereal onto a pipe cleaner and attach to a branch.

　❄ Spread peanut butter on a pinecone and sprinkle on birdseed.

　❄ Spread peanut butter or honey on a large pretzel and then sprinkle with seeds.

　❄ Cut shapes out of stale bread with cookie cutters and decorate with peanut butter and seeds.

Grow a Garden

Children will learn the parts of a plant as they observe, predict, and record.

Materials: grass seed (rye works well), potting soil, plain paper cups (without waxy coating), markers, spray bottle

How To:

1. Let children draw faces on their cups with markers.

2. Fill the cups half full with potting soil. Sprinkle grass seed on the dirt.

3. Water seeds with a spray bottle, then set the cups in a sunny window. Each day let a different child spray them with water. Have children predict how long it will take the grass to grow.

4. Encourage children to observe their "hairy" plants daily. Have them draw observations, measure the grass, and even give the gardens haircuts!

And...

❋ Ask children to go on a seed hunt in their kitchen at home. Plant the seeds they bring to school in small cups of potting soil and label each cup. (Apple seeds, lemon seeds, orange seeds, avocados, and so on can be used.) Ask, *What grows? What doesn't?*

❋ Have a "seedy" snack by eating sunflower seeds, popcorn, pumpkin seeds, pickles, grapes, and other foods with seeds.

❋ Put an old sock over your shoe and take a walk outdoors, somewhere with a lot of weeds. Place the sock in a clear, self-sealing bag. Wet the sock and punch a few small holes in the bag. Hang the bag in a window…and watch things grow!

What's Up?

Here's another old favorite that lets children observe how plants "drink" water.

Materials: two celery stalks (with leafy tops), two clear plastic glasses, food coloring

How To:

1. Place a stalk of celery in each glass of water.

2. Add red food coloring to one cup and blue to the other.

3. Have children predict what they think will happen. Record their observations.

4. Observe for several days. Plants use *capillary action* to carry food to their leaves and flowers.

And...

* Have children draw pictures of the results.

* Ask children to describe how they think water gets to the leaves in trees.

* Do the same experiment with white carnations, daisies, or yellow daffodils.

* Teach children the parts of a plant by singing the song below to the tune of "Head, Shoulders, Knees, and Toes."

Flower, *(hands around face)*
Stem, *(point to neck)*
Leaves, *(stick out arms)*
and roots. *(touch feet)*
Leaves and roots.
Flower, stem, leaves, and roots—
Leaves and roots.

All it takes is sun
(hands up in circle)
and showers,
(wiggle fingers down)
and a seed *(hold out palm)*
grows into a flower. *(spread fingers of right hand up from left fist)*

Litter Patrol

Build a sense of personal responsibility and awareness of conservation and recycling.

Materials: empty cereal boxes, string or yarn, hole punch, paint and brushes

How To:

1. Cut one end off the box. Punch a hole near the top on each side and tie on a piece of string long enough for a handle. Have children paint the boxes.

2. Children can use the boxes as "garbage cans" for their family's cars, or paper recycling boxes for car or home.

And...

❋ Ask, *What happens if people throw their trash out of their car window? How can they help keep Earth clean?*

❋ Explore the process of paper recycling by reading *Recycled Paper From Start to Finish* by Samuel G. Woods and Gale Zucker (Blackbirch, 2000).

Four Seasons

Teach the seasons and the concept of sequencing at the same time

Materials: paper plates (one per child), crayons or markers, rulers

How To:

1. Teach children the song below (to the tune of "Oh, Susannah!").

2. Give each child a paper plate and show children how to draw lines to divide it into quarters. Help them label each quarter and illustrate each season.

And...

✳ Select a nearby tree to be your "class tree." Have children name the tree and observe it throughout the year. Take photographs of the tree in different seasons and let children record the changes in the tree with drawings and stories.

Winter, spring, summer, fall,
Four seasons of the year.
Winter, spring, summer, fall,
I enjoy them all.

First comes winter,
with ice and with snow.
Don't forget your mittens
when the cold wind blows.

Next, comes spring
when the Earth warms up.
Birds sing and flowers bloom.
Wake up, buttercups!

Then it's summer,
with long, hot days.
Read, bike, swim
and in the sunshine play.

Finally, it's fall
and the earth cools down.
Leaves turn red, yellow,
orange, and brown.

Seasons, seasons, bring changes for all.
Winter, spring, summer, fall,
I enjoy them all.

Weather Wheel

Children observe, predict, record, and graph the weather!

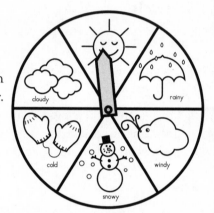

Materials: brad fasteners, pipe cleaners or cardboard, copies of page 27 (one per child; copy onto heavy paper)

How To:

Let each child color his or her a weather wheel and attach a pipe-cleaner or cardboard pointer with the brad fastener. Display one for circle time use. Sing the song below (to the tune of "BINGO") each day as children move the pointer on the appropriate weather. For instance, if it is sunny:

> There is some weather in the sky
>
> And sunny is its name-o.
>
> S – U – N – N – Y, S – U – N – N – Y,
>
> S – U – N – N – Y,
>
> And sunny is its name-o.

(Substitute *cloudy, humid, rainy, snowy, windy*, and so on in the song and spell out the words.)

And...

✳ Record the weather each day on a picture graph.

✳ Place a rain gauge outside to measure rainfall.

✳ Hang an outdoor thermometer outside the room and encourage children to look at it and predict if they will need to wear coats when they leave the building.

✳ Bring in a weather report from the newspaper. Ask, *What do you call someone who studies the weather?* (meteorologist)

✳ Demonstrate how to check the weather on the Internet. Ask children where grandparents or other relatives live and check the weather in those cities.

✳ Have children draw pictures of themselves in their favorite (or least favorite) type of weather.

Setting Up a **Math Center**

**A hands-on math center is an integral part of your classroom.
You'll want to stock it with all sorts of materials, such as**

* balance scale
* calculators
* chalkboard
* coins (US and foreign)
* computer
* counting books
* counting cubes
* Cuisinaire rods
* decks of cards
* dice

* dominoes
* flannel board and felt shapes
* games
* geoboard
* geometric shapes
* measuring cups and spoons
* minute timers
* number lines
* paper
* pattern blocks

* pencils
* play paper money
* play phone
* puzzles
* rulers
* sorting trays or boxes
* stopwatches
* tactile numerals and shapes
* tape measures
* toy clocks

Small Items to Use as Counters:

* acorns
* birthday candles
* buttons
* coins
* craft sticks
* crayons

* erasers
* hair bows or barrettes
* keys
* leaves
* marbles
* paint chips
* party favors

* pebbles
* shells
* small plastic toys
* toothpicks
* toy cars
* variety of dried beans
* variety of dry pasta

Math Center Tips

* Store materials in self-sealing bags, baskets, shoe boxes, or storage tubs. Label each container with the name and a picture of the item.

* Model how to use the materials as you introduce them.

* Begin by setting out one activity at a time. When children have learned how to use one activity and clean up, then add another. Children should have several choices but not be overwhelmed.

* Relate counters and math manipulatives to seasons or themes. For example, if you are doing an ocean unit, include shells to count and sort. In the fall, add nuts or leaves to the math center.

Meeting the Math Standards

The activities in this section align with the guidelines and teaching practices recommended in a joint position statement of the National Association for the Education of Young Children (NAEYC) and National Council of Teachers of Mathematics (NCTM).

In high-quality mathematics education for young children, teachers:

* enhance children's natural interest in mathematics and their disposition to use it to make sense of their physical and social worlds

* build on children's experience and knowledge, including their family, linguistic, cultural, and community backgrounds; their individual approaches to learning; and their informal knowledge

* base mathematics curriculum and teaching practices on knowledge of young children's cognitive, linguistic, physical, and social-emotional development

* use curriculum and teaching practices that strengthen children's problem-solving and reasoning processes as well as representing, communicating, and connecting mathematical ideas

* ensure that the curriculum is coherent and compatible with known relationships and sequences of important mathematical ideas

* provide for children's deep and sustained interaction with key mathematical ideas

* integrate mathematics with other activities and other activities with mathematics

* provide ample time, materials, and teacher support for children to engage in play, a context in which they explore and manipulate mathematical ideas with keen interest

* actively introduce mathematical concepts, methods, and language through a range of appropriate experiences and teaching strategies

* support children's learning by thoughtfully and continually assessing all children's mathematical knowledge, skills, and strategies

One-to-One Gummy Bears

Teach one-to-one correspondence, counting, money, and color recognition—with sweet treats!

Materials: red, yellow, orange, green, and purple construction paper; orange or brown poster board; markers

How To:

1. Cut five simple bear shapes from construction paper. Cut five circles from orange or brown poster board to use as "pennies."

2. Pass out the "gummy bears" to five children. Have them stand in a row in front of the group.

3. Pass out pennies to five other children. Tell them that they should stay sitting down until they hear their name in the song. When their name is sung, they should stand up and exchange their penny for the correct colored bear.

4. Continue singing with different numbers, children's names, and colors until each child has "bought" a gummy bear.

And...

* After each verse, stop and count how many bears and how many pennies.

* Vary the number of bears and colors. You might also let children use real coins to "buy" the bears.

Tune: "Six Little Ducks That I Once Knew"

Down at the candy store, what did I see?

Five little gummy bears smiling at me.
(Hold up five fingers.)

Along came _name_ with a penny one day.

Bought a _color_ one and took it away.

---

* Use real gummy bears.

* Have children match small animals and objects that go together on a flannel board (dogs and bones, flowers and pots, and so on).

* Give children opportunities for matching one-to-one with daily experiences in setting the table, passing out snacks, passing out pencils or books, and so on. Ask questions such as, *How many children are here today? How many spoons will we need?*

* Have children place tennis balls in muffin pans, plastic eggs in an egg carton, and so on.

Over in the Meadow

Reinforce numbers 1 through 5 using a traditional song.

Materials: none

How To:

Select different children to act out the animals in this song. You will need one child to be the mother, one child to be a frog, two children to be fish, three to be birds, four to be worms, and five to be bees.

And...

✳ Make a book illustrating different verses.

✳ Make up additional verses for numerals 6 through 10.

Over in the meadow
in the sand and the sun
lived a nice mother froggie
(Hold up one finger.)
and her little froggie one.
"Hop," said the mother.
"I hop," said the one.
So he hopped and was glad
in the sand and the sun.
(The "frog" begins hopping around the classroom.)

Over in the meadow
where the stream runs blue
lived a nice mother fishie
and her little fishies two.
(Hold up two fingers.)
"Swim," said the mother.
"We swim," said the two.
So they swam and were glad
where the stream runs blue.
(The two "fish" begin "swimming" around the room.)

Over in the meadow
in the nest in the tree
lived a nice mother birdie
and her little birdies three.

(Hold up three fingers.)
"Fly," said the mother.
"We fly," said the three.
So they flew and were glad
by the nest in the tree.
(The three "birds" pretend to fly.)

Over in the meadow
by the old apple core
lived a nice mother wormie
and her little wormies four.
(Hold up four fingers.)
"Squirm," said the mother.
"We squirm," said the four.
So they squirmed and were glad
by the old apple core.
(The four "worms" wiggle around.)

Over in the meadow
by the big beehive
lived a nice mother bee
and her baby bees five.
(Hold up five fingers.)
"Buzz," said the mother.
"We buzz," said the five.
So they buzzed and were glad
by the big beehive.
(The five bees "buzz" around.)

Ten in the Bed

Help children build skills in number recognition and addition and subtraction, while counting backward from, and forward to, 10.

Materials: copy of page 33, file folder, markers, scissors, tape, 9- by-14-inch piece of fabric, brad fastener

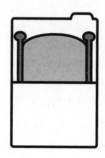

How To:

1. Color and cut out the pattern on page 33. Draw a headboard on the top half of an open file folder as shown. Attach the bears with a brad fastener.

2. Wrap the fabric around the bottom half of the file folder to look like a blanket and tape on the reverse side. As you sing the song at right, turn the "bear wheel" so that one bear disappears behind the fabric on each verse.

And...

❋ Have ten children act out the song.

❋ When you get to the end, reverse it:

> There was one in the bed,
> And the little one said,
> "I'm lonely. Come back."
> So he rolled over and
> One came back.
> There were two in the bed,
> And the little one said...

> There were ten in the bed,
> (*Hold up ten fingers.*)
> And the little one said,
> "It's crowded. Roll over."
> So they all rolled over,
> (*"Spin" one bear under the fabric.*)
> And one fell out.

> There were nine in the bed,
> (*Hold up nine fingers.*)
> And the little one said...
> (*Repeat until you reach one bear.*)

> There was one in the bed,
> And the little one said,
> "I'm tired. Good night!"
> (*Close folder.*)

Math

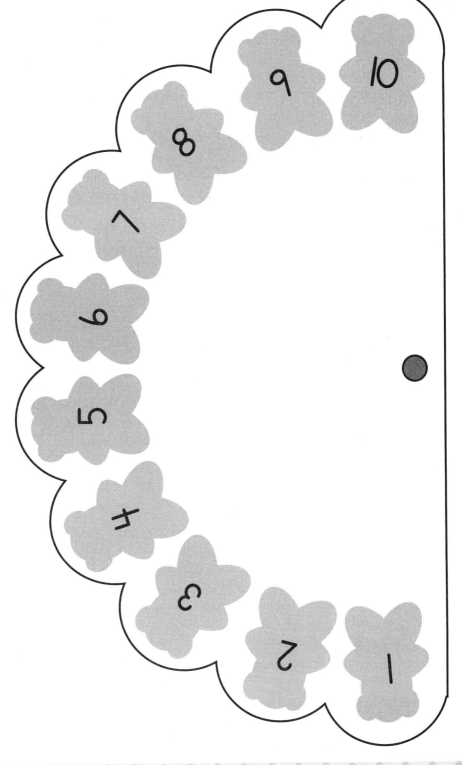

Show Me Cards

Use index cards to teach numeral recognition, sets, addition and subtraction, number stories, sequence, and place value.

Materials: index cards (11 per child), marker, self-sealing bags (one per child)

How To:

1. Make a set of cards for each child by writing the numerals 0 to 10 on the index cards.

2. Have children arrange their cards on the floor or a table in numerical order. Use the cards for any of the games below.

How Many?

Say, *Clap, snap, or stomp a number from 1 to 10. Show me the card with the numeral that tells how many. How many toes do you have? Show me the card with the numeral that tells how many.*

Sets

Say, *Make a set with felt pieces on a flannel board. Show me the card with the numeral that tells how many.* (You can also make sets on the overhead.)

Mystery Number

Say, for instance, *I'm thinking of a number between 4 and 6. Show me the card that tells the answer. Or, I'm thinking of a number 2 more than 7. Show me the card that tells the answer.*

Math Facts

Say, for instance, *4 plus 2. Show me the card that tells the answer. Or, 9 minus 3. Show me the card that tells the answer.*

Number Stories

Tell a story, such as *I had 4 pennies. I found 3 more. Show me the card that tells how many I have in all.*

And...

* "Show Me" cards can be used to reinforce almost any math skill you are working on. It involves all children and gives you the opportunity to quickly assess who has mastered a skill and who needs more help.

* Have children store their cards in a self-sealing bag.

* For younger children, start with the numbers 1 to 5 and add cards to meet their skill level.

Shell Tell

Teach sets, numerals, and number words—at the "seashore"!

Materials: ten white paper plates, markers, scissors

How To:

1. Fold the paper plates in half. Cut the edges so the plates resemble shells.

2. Draw sets of dots (you can also use stickers) on the front of the "shells" and write the corresponding numerals inside.

3. Demonstrate how to count the objects on the front, and then open the shell to verify the amount.

And...

* Write number words on the front and matching numerals inside.

* Write math facts on the front and answers inside.

* Write a series of numbers with a blank (such as *1, 2, ___, 4, 5*). Children guess the missing number (write it on the inside).

Stretchy Math

Give children practice matching sets and numerals.

Materials: heavy cardboard, markers, four rubber bands (in different colors, if possible)

How To:

1. From cardboard, cut rectangles with notches (see below).

2. Draw sets on one side and write numerals on the other side.

3. Children match correct sets and numerals with rubber bands. (On the reverse side, draw where rubber bands should be so children can self-check.)

And...

✳ Use this format to make similar games in which children match numerals with number words, math facts with answers, and so on.

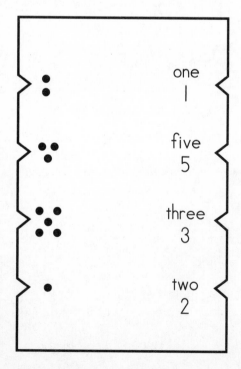

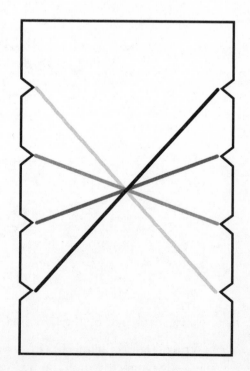

Macarena Math

Children build concepts of left and right as they practice counting to 12.

Materials: none

How To:

Build counting confidence by dancing the Macarena to the tune of "Ten Little Indians"!

And...

✳ Use this tune to count on fingers.

✳ Practice skip counting. Count by twos, fives, tens, and so on.

✳ Make an "I Spy" book. Assign each child a number from 1 to 12. Ask children to draw a set with that many objects on their paper. On each page, write "I spy (number of objects, name of objects)." Bind pages together into a book.

One,	*(Right hand out, palm up.)*
Two,	*(Left hand out, palm up.)*
Three,	*(Right palm down.)*
Four,	*(Left palm down.)*
Five,	*(Right hand on left shoulder.)*
Six,	*(Left hand on right shoulder.)*
Seven,	*(Right hand on back of head.)*
Eight,	*(Left hand on back of head.)*
Nine,	*(Right hand on left hip.)*
Ten,	*(Left hand on right hip.)*
Eleven,	*(Right hand on back of right hip.)*
Twelve,	*(Left hand on back of left hip.)*
Then we start again.	*(Sing and dance again.)*

✳ Teach children to "touch and count" as they count 12 objects in a picture, so they can grasp the concept of one-to-one correspondence. Otherwise, they may rote count and lose the concept of the quantity associated with different numbers.

Air Numerals

Here's a kinesthetic approach to numeral recognition and formation.

Materials: none

How To:

Sing the song below to the tune of "Skip to My Lou" as you practice writing invisible numerals in the air.

And...

* Writing numerals is challenging for many children. Sing this song often before asking them to make numerals on paper. Accept all attempts.

* So that both right- and left-handed children benefit, put the index finger from each hand together and use to make numerals.

* Try invisible writing with feet or elbows.

* Cut numerals from glitter, felt, yarn, sandpaper, and so on, and glue onto cardboard cards. Children can trace them as they sing.

* Have children use a wet sponge on the chalkboard to practice writing numerals.

1: Come right down and that is all. *(Use index and middle finger to do "invisible" writing in air. Keep elbow stiff.)*

Come right down and that is all.

Come right down and that is all,

to make the numeral 1! *(Pretend to "erase" numerals with palm between each verse.)*

2: Curve around and slide to the right . . .

3: Curve in and around again . . .

4: Down, over, down some more . . .

5: Down, around, put on a hat...

6: Curve in and around again...

7: Slide to the right and slant it down . . .

8: Make an "s," then close the gate . . .

9: Circle around then come right down . . .

10: Come right down, then make a zero . . .

We can sing the "Numeral Song," And make numerals all day long!

O-N-E Spells One

Build number word recognition and spelling skills with a fun song.

Materials: sentence strips, markers

How To:

Sing number words to the tune of "The Farmer in the Dell." Write number words on sentence strips and hold them up as you sing.

And...

* Make a book or song cards to go along with the song. Let children illustrate each verse. They might also make individual number books from blank books (on each page, have them write a word and numeral, then draw the corresponding number of objects).

* Make puzzles from number words. Cut paper plates in half. Write the word on one half and the numeral on the other half. Children can match words and numerals, then self-check.

* Lay out cards with number words. Have children use math manipulatives to make sets that reflect the number on each card.

O – n – e spells one. *(repeat)*
Spelling numbers is such fun.
O – n – e spells one.

T – w – o spells two. *(repeat)*
I can spell and so can you.
T – w – o spells two.

Three: It's as easy as can be.

Four: I can spell even more.

Five: I can spell and I can jive.

Six: Number words are a trick.

Seven: We're so hot we are sizzlin'.

Eight: We are smart. We spell great.

Nine: Spelling good and feeling fine.

Ten: You've spelled "ten" and that's the end.

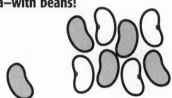

Math

Spill the Beans!

Teach sets, fact families, patterns, and algebra—with beans!

Materials: large, dry lima beans; nontoxic spray-paint; film canister or other small containers (one per child)

How To:

1. Spread the lima beans on newspaper and spray-paint on one side. Let dry.

2. Give each child ten beans to put in his or her container. Use the beans for some of the activities below.

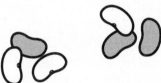

Addition and Subtraction

Pose simple addition and subtraction challenges, such as *Make a set of 3 and a set of 4. Put them together. How many in all?* Or, *Make a set of 9. Take 3 away. How many are left?*

Counting

Have children count their beans aloud. Or, write a numeral on chart paper and have them count out that number.

Sets

Challenge children to make sets of 2. They can also make sets of 5. Each time, ask, *How many pairs (or groups) do you have?*

Fact Families

Have children put 5 beans in their containers, shake them, then pour them out. Ask, *How many colored ones? How many white ones? How many in all?* Close and shake again. Again ask, *How many colored ones? How many white ones? How many in all?* Continue having children shake the beans to discover the different combinations of 5. Record their different combinations.

Patterns

Have children create patterns with their beans. Can they make an AB pattern? How about an AAB pattern?

The Shape Family

Help children recognize, name, and form shapes.

Materials: none

How To:

Make the hand and arm motions described as you sing the song at right to the tune of "I'm a Little Teapot."

And...

❋ Make shapes out of felt and place them on the flannel board as you sing.

❋ Challenge children to make shapes with their bodies on the floor. Take a picture of their body shape, and then put them together to make a book!

❋ Have a shape snack of circles (cookies), triangles (tortilla chips), squares (crackers), and rectangles (graham crackers).

I am mama circle, round like a pie.
(Make a circle over head with arms overhead.)

I'm baby triangle, three sides have I.
(Make a triangle with three fingers.)

I am papa square, my sides are four.
("Draw" a square in the air.)

I'm cousin rectangle, shaped like a door.
("Draw" a rectangle in the air.)

I am brother oval, shaped like a zero.
(Make an oval with arms overhead.)

I'm sister diamond, I sparkle and I glow.
(Put thumbs and index fingers together to make a diamond.)

We are the shapes that you all know.
Look for us wherever you go.
(Make circles with index fingers and thumbs and place around eyes.)

❋ Invite children to make collages out of construction paper cut into shapes, and cut sponges into shapes and use for printmaking.

❋ Let children practice making shapes on each other's backs with their fingers. See if they can name the shapes their friends draw.

❋ Play "I Spy" with shapes. For instance, *I spy something that is a circle.* Children name various objects in the room until someone names the one you are thinking of. That child then continues the game by saying, *I spy a...*

Math

The Money Song

Teach about coins and their value.

Materials: penny, nickel, dime, quarter (real or play coins), child-safe magnifying glass

How To:

1. Set out coins so all children can see. Pass them around and let children examine them with a magnifying glass. Encourage them to notice and discuss details. Ask, *How old is the coin? What do the words say? What pictures do you see?*

2. Teach children this song to the tune of "Shortnin' Bread." As you sing, point to the appropriate coin or have a child hold it up.

And...

✳ Enlarge pictures of coins and hold them up like signs as you sing.

✳ Have children do rubbings of coins. Place each coin under a sheet of paper and rub with the side of a crayon. Ask, *Who do you see? What is this coin worth?*

A penny's worth one cent.
(Hold up one finger.)

A nickel's worth five.
(Hold up five fingers.)

A dime's worth ten cents.
(Hold up ten fingers.)

A quarter's twenty-five.
(Open and shut one hand five times.)

(Chorus)
We use money to buy things at the store.

I count and count and count and then I count some more!

Lincoln's on one cent.
(Hold up one finger.)

Jefferson's on five.
(Hold up five fingers.)

Roosevelt's on ten cents.
(Hold up ten fingers.)

Washington's on twenty-five.
(Open and shut one hand five times.)

(Chorus)

A building's on one cent.
(Hold fingers as above.)

A building's on five.

A torch is on ten cents.

An eagle's on twenty-five.

(Chorus)

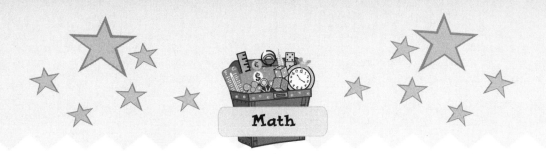

Bean Counters

Teach standard unit measurement with lima beans!

Materials: clear packaging tape; ten large, dried lima beans; ruler; scissors

How To:

1. Prepare these in advance, as the sticky tape is difficult for children to use. Lay a foot-long length of packaging tape on the table (sticky side up).

2. Place ten lima beans end to end on the tape. Fold up the bottom and top edge of the tape. Seal and trim off ends.

3. Use the "bean counter" to measure different objects in the classroom. Ask, *How many beans long is your little finger? How many beans long is a crayon?*

4. After children have measured objects, challenge them to find something in the room that is five beans long. Ask, *Can you find something three beans long? Eight beans long?*

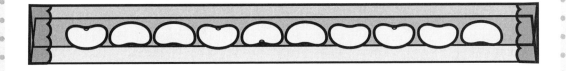

And...

* Ask, *How could we find out how long the classroom is?* Put the bean counters together and count by tens.

* Use the bean counters on the playground.

* Write the numerals 1 to 10 on the beans with a fine-tip permanent marker.

* Try standard unit measurement with paper clips, coins, blocks, crayons, and other classroom objects.

Hickory Dickory Dock

Children learn to tell time and recognize numerals with this favorite nursery rhyme.

Materials: classroom display clock

How To:

Teach children different verses to this traditional nursery rhyme.

And...

* Move the hands on the clock to show the times as you sing the song.

* Have twelve children sit in a circle and one child sit in the center. The child in the center will be the short and long hands on a clock (using arms and legs) and the children in the circle will represent the numerals on a clock. Call out various times for the "hands" child to create!

* Place a digital clock beside the traditional classroom clock so children can make the association between the two.

Hickory dickory dock.
(Fold hands and "tick" fingers back and forth.)

The mouse ran up the clock.
(Run fingers up in the air over head.)

The clock struck one,
(Clap one time.)

The mouse ran down.
(Run fingers down.)

Hickory dickory dock.

Additional Verses

Two: "Yahoo!" *(Continue doing movements listed above, clapping the appropriate number of times.)*

Three: "Whoopee!"

Four: "Do more!"

Five: "Let's jive!"

Six: "Fiddlesticks!"

Seven: "Oh, heavens!"

Eight: "Life's great!"

Nine: "So fine!"

Ten: "We're near the end."

Eleven: "We're sizzlin'."

Twelve: "I'm proud of myself."

Math

Estimation Bottle

Children love estimating and counting with the Estimation Bottle!

Materials: clear plastic bottle, small objects that fit in the bottle

How To:

1. Fill a plastic bottle with a set of small objects, such as marbles, small toys, erasers, crayons, small wrapped candies, and so on.

2. Pass around the bottle and ask each child to guesstimate how many there are. Record children's predictions.

3. Remove the objects and count them. Ask, *Who guessed more? Who guessed fewer? Who guessed the closest amount?*

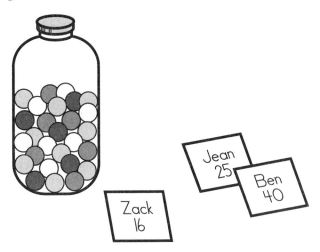

And...

✳ Put the estimation bottle on a table with a basket, pencil, and slips of paper. Children write their names and estimates and put them in the basket. At the end of the day, count and compare answers. Ask, *Who guessed closest? How many guessed a number higher than the actual number? How many guessed a number that was lower?*

✳ Make bottles for your "100th Day of School" celebration. Have each child fill a bottle with exactly 100 objects. Ask, *Whose is heaviest? Lightest? Whose object take up the most space?*

Great Graphs

Teach children to compare and record, while celebrating the similarities and differences among us.

Materials: graph paper, chart paper, or poster board; markers; crayons

How To:

Draw a grid similar to the one below. Let children color in the appropriate section of the graph.

How many letters?	1	2	3	4	5	6	7
Tim	▓	▓	▓				
Ericka	▓	▓	▓	▓	▓	▓	
Joel	▓	▓	▓	▓			
Latisha	▓	▓	▓	▓	▓	▓	▓
Uri	▓	▓	▓				
Beth	▓	▓	▓	▓			

And...

✳ You can also do "people" graphs and have children arrange themselves into groups based on a particular attribute.

✳ Glue photographs of children onto index cards. Have children use their pictures for graphing activities.

✳ Expose children to line graphs, picture graphs, bar graphs, and other visual representations.

Ideas for Graphs

- eye color
- hair color
- brothers and sisters
- letters in children's names
- books read
- birthday month
- favorite ice cream flavor
- favorite pet
- favorite book, author, character
- favorite song, rhyme
- favorite sports team
- teeth lost
- weather
- color of jelly beans in a bag
- type of shoe
- favorite center

Math Snacks

**There's so much children can learn during snacktime!
Try any of these ideas to whet children's appetite for math.**

Counting Mix

Materials: o-shaped cereal, raisins, pretzels, crackers, miniature marshmallows, and other small food items; self-sealing bag

Give each child a self-sealing bag. Have children count out a specified number of each item and put them in their bag. Shake and eat! You can also make a "100th Day of School" treat by using ten of ten different items.

Drawing and Eating Shapes

Materials: square crackers, round cookies, rectangular graham crackers, triangular nacho chips, paper plate, pencil, paper

Give each child a paper plate, pencil, and paper. Have children trace the plate onto their paper and then move the plate aside. Put a square cracker on their plate and have them draw a square on the plate that they drew. One by one, put the other objects on the plate and have them draw the shapes. Have children name the shapes as they eat them.

3-D Learning

Materials: cheese balls (spheres), marshmallows (cylinders), caramels (cubes), Bugles (cones)

Pass out one item at a time to children. Discuss the name and the characteristics of each shape. Ask, *What else comes in that shape?*

Pretzel Numerals

Materials: pretzel twists and sticks

Give each child several twists and sticks. Challenge children to make numerals with the pretzels by nibbling and breaking them!

Number, Please

Teach numeral recognition and help children memorize their phone numbers.

Materials: shower curtain liner or large poster board, permanent marker, flyswatter, scissors

How To:

1. Cut the shower curtain in half and draw a giant cell phone on it with permanent marker. Add a plus sign, a minus sign, and an equals sign, as shown.

2. Let children take the flyswatter and "swat" numerals as you call them out.

3. Once children have gotten the hang of it, have them "swat" out their phone numbers.

And...

✳ Teach children their phone numbers by singing them to the tune of "Twinkle, Twinkle, Little Star."

> 555-4994, 555-4994
>
> 555-4994 — I know my phone number.
>
> 555-4994, 555-4994

✳ Let children throw two beanbags onto the buttons of the phone. Add the numbers on which the bean bags have landed.